ARCHAEOMYTHOLOGY

Kathryn Dohrmann

Parisian Phoenix Publishing, Easton, Pennsylvania

PARISIANPHOENIX.COM

angel@parisianphoenix.com

parisianphoenixpublishing.substack.com

@parisianphoenixpublishing
/parisan-phoenix-publishing
/parisianphoenixpublishing
@parisianphoenix
/parisianphoenix.bsky.social

parisian phoenix
PUBLISHING

...THE PLACES I INHABIT AND THAT INHABIT ME...

FOR ED AND ADRIAN

TABLE OF CONTENTS

RESTORATION RIDGE

Walking the high ridge
Between ravines feels like
Stepping on bones
Of something old
What a glacier left
As it headed north
Melting into itself.

You descend to water
As ravines merge
In light and motion
Looking up
As from a well
To banked maples and basswoods
Is looking back
Ice and time and change.

Today's red honeysuckle
Accepts the camera's soft click
Mammoths
Before oaks
Cathedrals
A great silence
Before this one
Something pulls back
To make room for us.

TRUE

And makes one little room an everywhere.
John Donne

Key by key by key, the tuner
probes low to high.
The house holds quiet mind.

There's a window nearby,
an 8-over-12, with thin panes
called true divided lights.

The window has no storm or screen;
the thorny Blackhaw
sprawls against it,

the Blackhaw filled with sparrows.
In spring they are flowers.
In fall they are fruit.

Often melodious, they are
a Greek chorus for poems, naps,
a child practicing scales.

Today the rain plays *pianissimo.*
Sparrows and their little-bird throng
shelter close to the glass,

heads tilting into the room,
attuned to the tuner
guiding each key to its true sound.

ALLÉE
—After Beth Moon's photograph, *Avenue of Oaks*

*All art is a magic operation, or, if you prefer,
a prayer for a new image.* Charles Simic

i

A small town, an old-fashioned thunderstorm, witnessed from inside the house on Hazel. Suddenly, lightning rolls down the street. Not a bolt, but a ball, round, jagged, like the blade of a circular saw.

A storm door frames the girl watching the lightning as it tumbles by. Herself watching herself. The house is dark, though the lamp in her father's study trembles. She stands her ground. Prays that she keeps some lightning for later, for all the days of her long life, for times when she will need it.

ii

At the end of the American Civil War, her great-grandfather left the coast of the Frisian Sea and came to a new town in Iowa. There was land to be had, scoured of prairie peoples and plants, a canvas painted over. The street plan, rooted in right angles, appealed to his mason's sensibilities.

3

Numbered streets ran east-west. Named streets, north-south: Birch, Hickory, Cedar, Olive, Oak, and so on. Chestnut defined the center. On each side of every street a parkway planted with elms. Elm allées. These led down steep hills to the river, the Nishnabotna, which is where, a century later, her lightning ball would roll.

iii
By the time the girl is grown, the elms have achieved their characteristically graceful, vase-shaped canopies, branches touching side-by-side, reaching over the street. More than one hundred years old, more than one hundred feet tall. The elms are to the town as courthouse, library, bank.

Elms frame the girl as she leaves for the city. Like a slow-moving storm, Dutch elm fungus arrives, crossing the Atlantic when an Ohio furniture maker imports some logs. The disease is one these elms do not know. The town bereft, burning in the sun. The prairie lifts its head, sniffs the wind.

The girl does not return, but always, when there are thunderstorms, she imagines the lightning ball and her elms.

iv
An allée is an avenue is an aisle is an illusion. Elm allées are no more, but one can get a sense of them from *Avenue of Oaks*. Southern live oaks. Their converging lines distort perception, and in the distance the avenue appears to narrow. The eye is drawn to the vanishing point. The allée is shadow, silence, reverie.

The Avenue oaks lead us from the Big House — centerpiece of Oak Alley Plantation — to the Mississippi River. Far upstream, in the middle waters of the continent, the girl's river, the Nishnabotna, and the mother river, the Mississippi, inevitably become one.

v
Of trees, Wendell Berry writes: *their life's a benediction made, and is a benediction said, over the living and the dead.*

Benediction. Even allée elms, imposed on a not-blank slate. Even avenue oaks, planted and tended by the enslaved.

Still, we must pray for better. The girl is running to the vanishing point, toward lightning.

SHAW PRAIRIE / REMEMBERING 9/11

There was nothing
but motion, low bending
bluestems and brown-eyed

susans, ten-spot dragonflies
massed in migration, common
nighthawk's dart and wheel.

In a dying season, the feast—
sunflower, coneflower,
goldenrod—food and seed,

life and life to be. Psalms
for Ceres, her autumn hymns.
How patiently the sky waits,

how often the sun and moon
have come to watch small flowers
learn their own light.

ORIOLE

My afternoon nap turns into a party. At first,
only the cat and a maple branch pressing
against the screen. Somewhere on the branch,

between the leaves of sleep and wake, the oriole
arrives, his song so loud that everyone hears,
even the dead. Mary Oliver strides in,

fresh from the feathery fields, notebook at the ready.
Will you remember, she asks, my good birds?
Owl that reads the Book of Revelation, goldfinches

falling like wheels of fire? O, Mistress of Images,
how could we forget? Rachel Carson appears,
eyeing the cat. I warned you, she sighs,

of spring without birds. We bow to her courage.
Rachel and the cat purr, as if praying in their sleep.
Finally, here's Emily, attuned, as always,

to ecstasy, ballads, bards. She laments
that "hope is a thing with feathers" has become
a cliché. Tell me about it, Mary nods.

We all turn to the oriole, little melodeon.
His song feels like rain, like storms,
like wild, precious, spring.

THROUGH THE DOOR MARKED SUMMER

Late June, the mouse-gray time
when sun has set
and moon has not yet
risen, we find
fireflies.

The four-year-old gasps
Oh!
The five-year-old intones
like a preacher-man
Oh My God!
Wise-seven pronounces
Whoa!

Whoa it is.
Whoa is what we all say
to every flare
and blink.

Stars burn, grass grows
an owl calls.
The children dart
under oaks
voices flashing
Whoa!   *Whoa!*   *Whoa!*

NISHNABOTNA

The Nishnabotna divided
town from not-town.
When spring rains cascaded
in biblical torrents,
the Nishnabotna overflowed,
erasing cornfields,
pastures, country roads.

On bikes we watched
from the old highway bridge,
water roiling, inches below.
We'd point to the Widow Alpers'
white farmhouse, stranded
on a patch of green,
forbidden island,
sky-tattered.

In summer heat
the Nishnabotna shrank
to ribbons and spring-fed
pools. Black Angus
browsed under cottonwood,
silt-fed. Sedges
held high banks in place,
nodding to the wind.

We knew the cautionary tales—
child catching catfish,
toddler slipping out
an unlocked door,
wandering
sand bars and shallows,
stolen by deep and hungry holes.

I am told that on the day
my little dog and I
ran away from home,
they found us
down by the Nishnabotna.

NIGHTWALK, WITH DOG

We walk the web
of streets around
the house, where
gas lamps gleam
in fog-spun seas
and night is still
safe for a walker
and her dog. Calls
of migrating geese
sift down, plaintive
and we rise
to greet them
offer ourselves
to unseen travelers
who know the dark
who make it ring
who find their way home
using no compass
but the heart.

ANNIVERSARY POEM

Over the house
one-hundred-fifty-year oaks
limbs like hands

clasping wind as it flies
from a lake following
sun's set and rise

bending in its phases
to the moon:
let there be spaces

and many branches
distinct but keeping sway
over loam where roots

make a common
nervous system so these trees
breathe together sighing singing.

ERRAND/ERRANT

I've been sent to buy cookies—
generic with icing—
the kind my minister father enjoys.

I mean to go home, but instead of turning
at 18th, I continue on Olive as it passes
asphalt, gravel, dirt.

Loess Hills surround, emerald,
empty as Chinese landscapes;
skies are unmarked,

darkening, and I'm lost in reverie.
When I leave, the men are drawing close
to Phillies vs. Cards,

mother putters in her kitchen.
Here, I have the road in mind,
its longing, the way

it mimics hills in wavelike rise and fall,
flowing west to the Missouri,
pulsing like a blue heart.

Cookies notwithstanding, you know
I'm not going anywhere; it's more
the place, the luxury

of isolation, the sense of quiet,
wind, a band of Angus
climbing toward home.

ROSEMARY BLUE

Someone wanted them to live forever,
hefted them from first frost
to winter's indoor dreaming.
The rosemaries are shapeshifting,
transmuting, say, from shrub to fern
to elf, stem to frond
to hand, slim fingers reaching
for the window. This late January morning
pale flowers appear,
small blue ears
listening for cardinals to commence
their spring songs.

BLEU ROMARIN

Quelqu'un leur souhaitait une vie éternelle,
les a remontés de la première gelée
aux rêves d'hiver au foyer.
Les romarins changent de forme,
se transmutent, disons, de buisson en fougère
en lutin, de tige en fronde
en nain, leurs doigts minces s'étendant
vers la fenêtre. Ce matin de fin de janvier
des fleurs pâles apparaissent,
tendant de petites oreilles bleues
pour capter les premiers chants
printaniers du cardinal.

Translation—Cynthia T. Hahn

BUR OAK ELEGY

Cedar waxwings
west-facing
high in the bare-branched

oak
lamplighters
from a forgotten age

the Waxwing Constellation
risen on dark moon's
eve

It takes a setting sun
a dying tree golden
breasts

something to say
Look up!
Look up!

MOWER BETTER BLUES

How can you mow in the dark?
she asks as I take her call,
wet grass dripping

from my shoes. Cutting at night,
I say, is like conversation:
the mower stutters

where going is thick;
when blades sing you know
you've been there. You can listen

to fresh cuts flurry.
Patience, letting it lead,
asking shadows

for what you've missed.
Lawns forgive quickly —
morning brings second chances.

SHE SAID

(for Lisel Mueller)

A well-known, nearly blind poet
came for lunch and stayed the day.
She said *I started out as a girl without a shadow,*
in iron shoes. All afternoon,
summersweet's fragrant fingers
crept through kitchen windows,
pinned us to the table.

Now, at the end of the world she said
I am a woman full of rain. She paused
a long moment in the doorway,
listening to the garden's blooming,
buzzing confusions — murmurs of bees
and cutting wings, labors
of roots and smallest things.

She said *what happens, happens in silence.*
Yes — and here it happened
in darkness behind her eyes,
beyond the inner ear, in cadences
not yet spoken, not yet heard.
She said *we are covered in stars.*

ARCHAEOMYTHOLOGY

Say tonight the world ends, collapses
like a dying star, unfolds. No one
for a thousand, ten thousand years.
Say that our bones settle, comfortable
heaps, our human bones, relaxed
bony mounds, dogs with us. Say
when they come, as they will —
digging, prying — they'll find
a circle of stones, tell-tale
hoops and here, with our bones,
jewelry, powders, female
accouterments. Archaeomythologists
will speculate, hypothesize.
Will they know we sang like loons,
howled like wolves, drummed and danced
antiphonies with a cycling moon?
Perhaps one among them, one
dimly imagined, will get it right,
will say: women, drummers. They
kept dogs, honored fire, loved the moon.

Acknowledgments

Gratitude—

To my supportive fellow writers and teachers: Lois, Cynthia, Karin, Ben, Tim

To Mirabel, Agustin, and Sebastian, for the firefly night, and Phoebe, for knowing that hope is a thing with feathers

To Beth Moon, for inspiration and generosity

To Angel Ackerman and Gayle Hendricks at Parisian Phoenix, for trust, skill, and imagination

To the hardworking editors of the journals where several of these poems appeared

About the Author

Kathryn Dohrmann has taught for many years in both the Psychology and Environmental Studies Departments at Lake Forest College. Her poems have been published in *CALYX; A Journal of Art and Literature by Women, The Chicago Tribune, The A-3 Review, The Ekphrastic Review, The Last Stanza Poetry Journal, OPEN; Journal of Arts & Letters*, and others. A finalist in the Gwendolyn Brooks Open Mic and WBEZ poet laureate competitions, she was also a participant in the Poetic Dialogue Project; her poems from that project — The Pandora Memos — have been anthologized in *Collaborative Vision* and *All About Eve*.

Notes

Archaeomythology: The title of this collection is inspired by the work of Marija Gimbutas (1921-1994). A prolific author and scholar, Gimbutas was controversial in professional archeological circles. Her final English-language books—*The Goddesses and Gods of Old Europe* (1974), *The Language of the Goddess* (1989), and *The Civilization of the Goddess* (1991)—have been formative for me.

The poem, "Archaeomythology," appeared in *Calyx; A Journal of Art and Literature by Women* (2009). Vol. 25 (1).

Epigraph: These words are paraphrased from Robert MacFarlane's moving interview with Barry Lopez, a few months before Lopez died.
Robert MacFarlane, *Orion*, March 30, 2023. "Geography as Generosity: An Afternoon with Barry Lopez." https://orionmagazine.org/article/barry-lopez-from-here-to-the-horizon/?mc_cid=d6958307f3&mc_eid=7455a03774

"Allée" was published in *Open; Journal of Arts and Letters* in 2024: https://ojalart.com/poetry-all-forms-stylesprose-poetrykathryn-dohrmannallee/.
The Nishnabotna River, which flows near my childhood home, is mentioned in some of these poems. The name, "Nishnabotna," was used by the First Nations of the southwest region of what is now called Iowa: the Dakotas, Sioux, Iowas, Osages, Missouris, Otoes, Omahas, and others. It likely means something akin to "crossed in a canoe" – referring to the river's width and depth. Lewis and Clark described the Nishnabotna River and its beautiful valley in their 1804 journals. https://pubs.lib.uiowa.edu/annals-of-iowa/article/9677/galley/118316/view/

Image: Beth Moon, *Allée*. Fine art photograph published in her collection, *Ancient Trees, Portraits of Time* (Abbeville Press 2014). By permission.
https://bethmoon.com/

The epigraph is from Charles Simic's prose poem, "A Force Illegible." *Dime-Store Alchemy, The Art of Joseph Cornell,* New York Review of Books, 1992.

From Wendell Berry's seven years of tree sabbaths, three lines of an untitled poem that begins "slowly, slowly, they return." *Sabbaths*, North Point Press, 1987.

The Last Stanza Poetry Journal published "Restoration Ridge" (Issue 17, 2024), "Nishnabotna" and "Errand/Errant" (Issue 15, 2024), "Nightwalk, With Dog" (Issue 12, 2023), and "Oriole" (Issue 9, 2022).

Nature Folklore was an Irish network created by the late woodland bard, John Willmott. I read the poem, "Through the Door Marked Summer," on his June 27, 2022, broadcast (at about the 28-minute mark).

East on Central published "Rosemary Blue" and "She Said" in Volume 15, 2016-2017. The French translation of "Rosemary Blue" is by Cynthia T. Hahn, a colleague at Lake Forest College. The italicized phrases in "She Said" are from the poems of Lisel Mueller (1924-2020), who lived out on the edge of my town. In 1997, she won the Pulitzer Prize for her poetry collection, *Alive Together: New and Selected Poems.* "She Said" also has hints of Margaret Wise Brown.

"Mower Better Blues" appeared in the *Chicago Tribune* (August 16, 2004).

www.ingramcontent.com/pod-product-compliance
Lightning Source LLC
Chambersburg PA
CBHW051253120626
46547CB00014B/1929